THE
SANTEE SIOUX
INDIANS

THE JUNIOR LIBRARY OF
AMERICAN INDIANS

THE
SANTEE SIOUX
INDIANS

Terrance Dolan

CHELSEA JUNIORS

a division of CHELSEA HOUSE PUBLISHERS

FRONTISPIECE: This map shows where different bands of the Santee Sioux tribe lived in what would later become the Minnesota Territory. After the failed Sioux uprising of 1862, the Santees were driven from their beloved "Big Woods" almost entirely.

CHAPTER TITLE ORNAMENT: This symbol for a deer appears in the art of native groups from the southwestern United States.

English-language words italicized in the text can be found in the glossary at the back of the book.

Chelsea House Publishers

EDITORIAL DIRECTOR Richard Rennert
ART DIRECTOR Sara Davis
PRODUCTION MANAGER Pamela Loos
PICTURE EDITOR Judy Hasday

Staff for THE SANTEE SIOUX INDIANS
SENIOR EDITOR Martin Schwabacher / Jane Shumate
ASSOCIATE EDITOR Therese De Angelis
EDITORIAL ASSISTANT Kristine Brennan
DESIGNER Takeshi Takahashi
PICTURE RESEARCHER Sandy Jones
COVER ILLUSTRATOR Bradford Brown

First Printing

1 3 5 7 9 8 6 4 2

Library of Congress Cataloging-in-Publication Data

Dolan, Terrance.
The Santee Sioux Indians/ Terrance Dolan.
     p.   cm.—(The Junior Library of American Indians)
Includes index.
Summary: Examines the history and present status of the Santee Sioux Indians, discussing their fight to maintain their native lands under the leadership of Chief Little Crow.
ISBN   0-7910-1671-4 (hc)
            0-7910-4453-X (pbk)
1. Santee Indians—History—Juvenile literature. 2. Santee Indians—Land tenure—Juvenile literature. 3. Santee Indians—Government relations—Juvenile literature. [1. Santee Indians. 2. Indians of North America—Great Plains.] I. Title. II. Series.
E99.S22D65 1996
977.6'004975—dc20
                                                                    96-25065
                                                                    CIP
                                                                    AC

CONTENTS

Thirty-eight Santee Sioux Indians accused of taking part in a violent uprising against white settlers are executed by hanging in Mankato, Minnesota, in 1862.

CHAPTER 1

The Moon When the Deer Shed Their Horns

In 1862, 300 Santee Sioux Indians were sentenced to death by hanging for taking part in a brief but furious uprising that left 400 white settlers in Minnesota dead. But the 300 Santees had been allowed none of the legal rights promised to American citizens in the *Constitution* and the *Bill of Rights*, which are the documents that were drawn up when the nation was founded to establish the principles of freedom, law, and justice in the new United States. Unfortunately, the Constitution and the Bill of Rights did not consider the rights of the

7

people who already inhabited the land that the new nation would rest upon.

For centuries before European explorers set foot in North America, the region had been the homeland of a great number of peoples, tribes, and nations. An estimated 500 Indian nations, including the Santee Sioux of present-day Minnesota, had existed on the lands that would eventually become the United States of America. Over a period of about 150 years beginning in the late 1700s, these lands would be taken from their original inhabitants by white newcomers, who would also attempt to destroy the culture of the American Indians.

In the summer of 1862, the Santees who staged the violent uprising in Minnesota were fighting to win back lands that had gradually been taken over by white American settlers. Because the Santees were not American citizens, however, they were not protected by the Constitution and the Bill of Rights. This meant that, in the eyes of the law, they had no real claim to the lands they fought for.

Originally, 300 Santees were sentenced to death by hanging for taking part in the uprising. Upon reviewing the case, however, President Abraham Lincoln decided that many of the trials had been unfair and so reduced the number of death sentences to 38. Those 38 were executed on December 26—in the month known to the Santees as the Moon When the Deer Shed Their Horns. The hangings took place before a huge crowd on a giant wooden gallows built for the occasion in the town of Mankato, Minnesota.

The condemned Santees held hands and chanted their death chants as the nooses were slipped around their necks. They were all hanged at the same moment. The mass hanging was the largest occasion of *capital punishment* in the history of the United States. Of the 300 who had originally been sentenced to death, those who were not executed were given long prison terms. Many of those who were hanged had not participated in the uprising and were innocent of any crime. Later, when the government learned that several innocent men had been executed, spokesmen commented that this was "regrettable."

Not all of those who participated in the uprising were captured, however. Chief Little Crow, the leader of the uprising, escaped with a band of followers to Canada. Many participants fled westward onto the Great Plains and joined their cousins, the Teton Sioux, who, for the time

being, were too strong and fierce for U.S. military forces to subdue.

Still other Santees scattered in various directions, alone or in small groups. Many disappeared into the Big Woods of Minnesota, and some joined other tribes. The remainder of the Santee Sioux—about 2,000 men, women, and children—were rounded up and placed in a prison camp at

About 2,000 Santees lived in this prison camp in Fort Snelling, Minnesota, for nearly a year after the uprising of 1862. They then were taken by boat to the badlands of Dakota Territory.

Fort Snelling, Minnesota. These Santees had committed no crimes, but as they passed through towns in Minnesota on their way to the fort, they were attacked by mobs of white people. The caravan of creaking wagons was escorted by U.S. soldiers, but they could not protect the captive Santees from flying stones and swinging sticks, and many of the Indians were injured.

But the hangings and imprisonments did not satisfy the white citizens of Minnesota. They demanded that every Santee Sioux be either killed or forever removed from Minnesota. The white settlers of Minnesota were determined never again to face such an uprising. The U.S. government thought removal of the entire tribe was a good idea as well. Removing the Santees not only eliminated the risk of more violence between settlers and the Santees but also provided a solution to the problem of

The barren, hostile terrain of the Dakota badlands seemed unlivable after Minnesota's woods and waters. Many Santees died in the brutal new environment, and their bodies were ceremoniously placed in trees or on scaffolds like this until the ground had thawed enough to allow burial.

acquiring the remaining Santee Sioux lands in Minnesota.

In May 1863, those Santee Sioux who had been held at Fort Snelling were herded onto a steamboat and taken up the Missouri River to the town of Hannibal, Missouri. There they were crowded into railroad boxcars for the final leg of the journey into exile. The train brought the Santees to the harsh badlands of the Dakota Territory. When the train stopped and the boxcar doors opened, the Santees looked about in horror.

A *reservation* had been chosen for the Santees at a place called Crow Creek. Here the exiles might as well have been on the surface of the moon. The jagged, rocky landscape held no trees, no drinkable water, no fertile soil for planting, no houses, and no wildlife. Here, amid the desolation of Crow Creek, the Santees would be forced to make a new home for themselves. Thinking of the difference between the beautiful Big Woods of Minnesota and this barren land, many of the Santees wept.

All of the hundreds of thousands of American Indians across the continent who were confined to reservations suffered greatly. But none suffered more than the Santee Sioux during their two years at Crow Creek. Starvation, disease, and exposure to the harsh elements in that desolate place killed them by the hundreds. The reservation became surrounded by graves.

With their homeland gone, their tribe broken and scattered to the winds, many of their people imprisoned or dead, and still others in hiding, the Santee Sioux faced a bleak future. Soon, even their culture, their religion, and their way of life were under attack by the forces of the white "civilization" that was overrunning the continent. The following words, left behind by a nameless and hopeless Indian, express the feelings that many of the Santees must have felt at Crow Creek:

My sun is set. My day is done. Darkness is stealing over me. Hear me, for this is not the time to tell a lie. The Great Spirit made us, and gave us the land. He gave us the buffalo, antelope, and deer for food and clothing. . . . We were free as the winds and heard no man's commands. . . . Our children were many and our herds of horses were large. Our old men talked with spirits and made good medicine. Our young men hunted and made love to the girls. Where the tipi was, there we stayed, and no house imprisoned us. No one said, "To this line is my land, to that line is yours." Then the white man came to our hunting grounds, a stranger. We gave him meat and presents, and told him to go in peace. But his fellows came to build their roads across our hunting grounds. He brought the mysterious iron that shoots. He brought with him the magic water that makes men foolish. With his trinkets and beads he even bought the girl I loved. I said, "The white man is not a friend, let us kill him." But their numbers were greater than blades of grass. They took away the buffalo and shot down our best warriors. They took away our lands and surrounded us by fences. Their soldiers came with cannon to shoot us down. They wiped the trails of our people from the face of the prairies. They forced our children to forsake the ways of their fathers. When I turn to the east I see no dawn.   When I turn to the west approaching night hides all. ▲

Seth Eastman's "Sioux Indians Breaking Camp." Like other Sioux peoples, the Santees moved their villages according to the season, living sometimes in tipis made of hide and sometimes in light wooden houses. Santee women were responsible for taking down the tipis (which were considered their property), packing up the household goods, and reassembling their homes at the new village site.

1CHAPTER 2

"Free as the Winds"

"Darkness is stealing over me," the unknown and despairing Indian wrote as he faced the twilight of his people's culture. But circumstances had not always been so desperate for the Santee Sioux. Before the coming of the white people, the Santees had indeed been, in the Indian writer's words, as "free as the winds." For hundreds of years they had flourished in the deep forests and rich countryside of Minnesota.

Originally, the Sioux (pronounced like the name Sue) were a single large tribe living in the northern reaches of Wisconsin and the

17

eastern regions of the Canadian provinces of Ontario, Manitoba, and Saskatchewan. But the Sioux had been driven southward and then westward by the huge and hostile Ojibwa nation. When the Sioux reached the Minnesota River, they split up. Part of the tribe kept moving west, onto the Great Plains of North Dakota, South Dakota, Montana, Wyoming, and northern Nebraska. This group split again, into two groups that remained on the Great Plains: the Teton Sioux and the Yankton Sioux.

The group of Sioux who did not journey westward onto the plains settled in the valley of the Minnesota River, often camping near Knife Lake. Because the Sioux word for knife was *isanti*, they became known as the Santee Sioux.

The Santees called their territory the Big Woods. Within the deep forests of Minnesota were many rivers, streams, lakes, and wetlands. The region also held rolling prairies to the west. In this land of abundant natural resources, the Santees acquired all the food they needed through hunting, gathering, and agriculture. They planted crops such as corn, beans, sweet potatoes, and squash and harvested wild rice, which grew in the marshes. They gathered wild berries, fruit, roots, and herbs.

They hunted buffalo on the prairies or along the outer edges of the forest, and in the shadowy woods they tracked elk, deer, moose, bear, rabbit, badger, and pheasant. From the lakes, streams, and rivers they hauled trout and other fish. And they collected the sap of maple trees, boiled it, and allowed it to harden into sweet maple sugar.

Once they had permanently settled in the Minnesota River valley region, the Santee tribe divided into four divisions: the Wahpekutes ("shooters among the leaves"), Sissetons ("campers among the marshes"), Wahpetons ("dwellers among the leaves"),

As depicted in this painting by Seth Eastman, the Santees' territory in present-day Minnesota was forested and full of lakes and streams, from which the Indians fished to round out a diet of fruit, vegetables, rice, and game.

and Mdewakantons ("people of Spirit Lake").
The four divisions were closely tied and
often visited each other. Many people married members of other divisions, and family
groups from different divisions often joined
together for long periods of traveling and
hunting.

Each of the four divisions of the Santees
consisted of several bands, which themselves were made up of a number of
tiyospaye—the basic family unit of Santee
society. A tiyospaye was an extended family group that usually included the head-
man, or leader, his wife, children, parents,
grandparents, in-laws, cousins, uncles,
aunts, and sometimes very close friends
and their families.

After settling in Minnesota, the Santees
continued to raid and skirmish with their traditional enemies to the north, the Ojibwa.
Often warriors from different divisions
joined together to form war parties for these
raids. The Santees occasionally battled
other tribes that ventured into Santee territory, such as the Crees, the Sacs, and the
Hurons. But their warfare was usually on a
minor scale, with small bands of warriors
engaging in ritual raids and displays of
courage. They suffered few casualties. On
the other hand, the Santees' fierce cousins,

the Teton Sioux, waged a relentless war of conquest on the northern Great Plains and eventually dominated most of that vast territory. Compared with the Tetons, the Santees were fairly peaceful. They developed friendly relations with most neighboring tribes, such as the Cheyennes, Mandans, Arikaras, and Hidatsas. The Santees traded for various foods and goods with these tribes.

The Santees, like the other Sioux peoples, tended to be tall and strong. Men wore deerskin breechcloths, leggings, and shirts, as well as moccasins of deer or buffalo skin. Women wore long shirts and leggings. The Santees wrapped themselves in heavy buffalo-hide robes in the winter. Their clothing was decorated with paint and with dyed porcupine quills sewn into a design. Both men and women wore their black hair long. Men cut their hair into bangs on their foreheads and allowed the rest of their hair to grow long and free, while Santee women wore their hair extremely long and twisted it into two braids. Both male and female Santees painted their faces, making their coal-dark eyes and strong facial structure even more prominent. Young women, for example, might paint a small red dot on their foreheads, where their hair was parted.

They might also paint a red dot on each of their high cheekbones. Men used much more paint on their faces, drawing streaks and designs or painting entire portions of their faces a certain color. Both men and women liked to wear bracelets, necklaces, and other ornaments fashioned from shells, smooth rocks, and animal claws and teeth. Once they had met white European explorers and traders, their adornments included trinkets, jewelry, military decorations, and even hats, buttons, handkerchiefs, boots, and other articles obtained through trade or taken from white soldiers or settlers killed in battle. Headdresses fashioned from colorful feathers were often worn by Santee men.

The Big Woods was a place of great beauty, freedom, and resources for the Santees, but it was also a formidable and unforgiving environment that required expert wilderness skills to survive. Dangerous animals roamed the forests. A hostile war party might raid at any time. Winters were harsh and frigid, with blizzards that could last for a week or more. But the Santees survived and prospered. Daily life in the Big Woods conditioned them to be strong, agile, and alert. All of the Sioux peoples, including the Santees, were renowned for their ability to endure hardship and physical discomfort

Karl Bodmer's "Indians Hunting the Bison." Once European explorers had brought horses to the American continent, Native Americans had a new way of hunting. Although the Santees' principal home was in the woods of Minnesota, they also hunted bison on the neighboring prairies.

without complaint.

Childhood for Santee boys and girls was a time of excitement, exploration, long days of play, and little discipline. Serious punishment was rarely needed because Santee children learned what was expected of them at an early age. They knew that any misbehavior on their part might cause a problem not only for themselves but for the entire community. For example, as infants, Sioux quickly learned not to cry, especially when they were traveling. The cries of a child could draw the attention of hostile warriors or dangerous animals such as grizzly bears, or they could scare away game that might have been hunted for food.

Children learned their roles in Santee society by observing their elders and by playing games that mimicked the roles they would assume as adults. Boys held hunting contests, swimming, climbing, and running races, bow-and-arrow competitions, wrestling matches, and other tests of the strength, stealth, agility, and survival skills needed for life in the Big Woods. Girls learned the roles of Santee women, who did everything from gathering berries and harvesting wild rice in the wetlands to preserving foods and preparing meals. Santee women were also responsible for embroidering buffalo robes and other clothing, constructing tipis, and making comfortable home environments inside the tipis. Although no formal schooling existed, Santee children spent many hours listening to elderly members of their tiyospaye tell tales of great warriors, significant events, admirable Santee women, and the many spirits and supernatural creatures that were both worshiped and feared by the Santees. In this manner, Santee children were taught the traditions, spirituality, and history of their people.

Romance among Santee men and women was a private affair marked by shyness and modesty. A young man might signal his interest in a young woman by a simple, meaningful glance into her eyes. Exchanges of smiles and hurried but affectionate words of greeting might then be exchanged when the two Santees encountered each other during the day's activities. The young man might then be encouraged enough to offer a small gift to the woman. He might sit within the dark woods at night in a place near the woman's tipi and play a love song on a carved wooden flute. Eventually, if all went well, the young Santee woman would simply move into the tipi of the young man, becoming his wife and a member of his tiyospaye. Months later, the marriage would be celebrated by the entire band or tribe. Sometimes, on the other hand, parents would arrange marriages. But if a marriage was unsatisfactory to either partner, he or she broke the union by simply moving out of the home.

The society of the Santees was communal. No individual member of the Santee community considered himself or herself more important than the group as a whole. Even leaders of the tribe were not considered more important than the community. A

chief, therefore, did not command his people unless they allowed him to. Santee leaders could only offer advice. They could not
give orders. The Santees believed that tribal well-being would ensure the well-being of
each person within the tribe. Therefore,
individuals who acted in the best interests
of the entire community were also acting in
their own best interests. This philosophy
enabled the Santees to thrive as a community and to thrive as individuals as well.

The tradition of the *giveaway* exemplifies

Santee life was deeply communal. This meant that no one considered himself or herself more important than the group, and even very young children quickly learned how to behave so as not to disturb the well-being of the community.

the Santees' communal philosophy and the value they placed on generosity. An event of special importance, such as a marriage, a successful hunt or battle, or the birth of a child, was often celebrated with a giveaway. According to this tradition, the people who were the cause for celebration—the newly married couple, the couple who had just had a child, the successful hunter or great warrior, the young man recently named to a position of leadership in the tribe—would, instead of receiving gifts for their good fortune, give gifts away. In this manner, the gift giver would share his or her good fortune with the entire community. The giveaway tradition reinforced community bonds. It also reflected favorably on the gift giver, strengthening his or her stature as an individual within the community.

Santee leaders were chosen because they possessed and displayed the four great virtues of Sioux culture: bravery, fortitude, generosity, and wisdom. Leaders included headmen of tiyospayes; Shirt Wearers, who were tribal spokesmen and wore distinctive white shirts; Pipe Bearers, tribal counselors whose duties included carrying sacred ceremonial pipes; and Whip Bearers, who enforced tribal rules and laws. Each of the four divisions of Santees also had a chief, and there were lesser chiefs for the bands within the divisions. Many chiefs were the sons of previous chiefs. But a chief only commanded as much respect and power as he earned through his actions, character, and practice of the four virtues. Many great Sioux leaders, such as the famous Teton leader Crazy Horse, had no official rank or title. But these leaders were so brave, wise, generous, and dedicated to their people's well-being that they commanded more respect and held more power than any officially ranked Shirt Wearer, Pipe Bearer, or chief.

The most important aspect of Santee Sioux culture was spirituality. This spirituality was most evident in the Santees' respect for the natural world around them. The environment of the Big Woods—including the weather, the seasons, the four winds, the lakes, streams, and rivers, the abundant wildlife, the sun, moon, and stars, the blades of grass and the very earth they grew upon, and the Santees themselves— was all a part of the Great Spirit, also known as *Wakan Tanka*, or the "Great Mysterious." Wakan Tanka was the universal life force, whose energy and spirit shone through all things. The timber wolf moving silently through the snowy forest at twilight, the hoot of the owl at night, the rays of golden sunlight that slanted through the trees of the Big Woods, the clear streams and icy lakes, and even the stones that lay on the ground held spiritual meaning for the Santees. So, also, did the smallest and most routine activities of daily life.

Because the Santees believed their natural environment to be the manifestation of Wakan Tanka, they never considered themselves superior to nature, for this would mean that they were superior to Wakan Tanka. For the Santees, it was sinful to damage the natural environment or to take more from it than was needed, because doing such things would be the same as assaulting Wakan Tanka. The Santees believed that their existence in the Big Woods was a gift, something to give thanks for and to celebrate in the thoughts and activities of their daily life. These beliefs allowed the Santees to lead an existence of heightened spiritual awareness, deeply in tune with their natural environment. Like the timber wolf, the Santee Sioux were simply another part of the Big Woods. And, like the timber wolf, they would one day become an endangered species. ▲

This painting by Frank Blackwell Mayer depicts one of the treaty conferences between Sioux Indians and white representatives of the United States government. At this meeting, which took place at Traverse des Sioux in 1849, the Santees sold 21 million acres of land in exchange for a small reservation and the promise of annual payments.

CHAPTER 3

"A Great Quantity of Money"

"I was to receive a great quantity of money every year," said the Santee Sioux named Standing Buffalo. "The money left the hands of (the president of the United States) but in passing from hand to hand, each one taking his part, nothing reached my hand more than a dollar. My heart was sad in seeing that."

Standing Buffalo may not have known it, but he was repeating an old story. Whites of European descent—first explorers, then colonists and settlers, and finally new Americans—had been making and later

31

breaking treaties and promises with the original inhabitants of North America since the Pilgrims had arrived at Plymouth Rock. As the population of white Americans swelled, the newcomers pushed relentlessly westward in a quest for land and the continent's rich resources. The fact that these lands were already inhabited meant little to the new Americans.

Most Indian peoples were eventually obliged to go to war to save their lands, for to lose their lands was to lose their culture and even their souls. A Sioux named Standing Bear wrote of the Indians' love of the earth itself: "They sat on the ground with the feeling of being close to a mothering power. It was good for the skin to touch the earth, and the old people like to remove their moccasins and walk with their bare feet on the sacred earth. The soil was soothing, strengthening, cleansing and healing."

For the Indians, a person could not own the earth any more than a person could own the air or the sunshine or a blessing from Wakan Tanka. But the whites wanted to own the land and say, "This part of the earth belongs to me, and therefore I can treat it as I wish and you cannot hunt or live here anymore."

"The greatest object of their lives seems to

Instead of going to meet Native Americans in their territories to negotiate for land, the federal government sometimes brought the Indians to Washington —perhaps to impress them with the capital's size and power. This photograph of a Sioux delegation that came to Washington in 1858 shows some of the more superficial ways that white and Indian cultures clashed.

be to acquire possessions—to be rich,"
Standing Bear wrote about the white people. "They desire to possess the whole
world." The famous Santee Sioux physi-
cian, educator, writer, and orator known as
Charles Eastman (his Santee name was
Ohiyesa) wrote of the fundamental difference between white and Indian cultures:
"(White civilization is) a system of life based
on trade. The dollar is the measure of
value, and might spells right." "To have,"

wrote Eastman, was the motto of white civilization.   "To be" was the motto of the American Indian.

The white newcomers felt that they were superior to the Indians because they were Christians and the Indians were not. They believed that they had the right to take the land from the Indians and use it as they thought it should be used—for farming. They also believed that they had the right to force the Indians to adopt white, Christian culture, which of course meant destroying tribal culture. But Eastman believed that the Indians were in fact more truly spiritual than the white Christians.   He noted that Christians set aside one day a week for spiritual activities, while Indians, on the other hand, worshiped every day. In the Santee Sioux culture, wrote Eastman, "every act of life [was], in a very real sense, a religious act."

In the end, such profound differences could not be resolved peacefully. The new Americans were determined to take control of the traditional homelands of different Indian tribes across the continent. And the Indians, when all else failed, were forced to defend their homelands and their culture. And so they fought, in the woodlands of the Atlantic coast, in the Appalachian regions of

Pennsylvania and Ohio and Kentucky, in the Southeast, in the Great Lakes territory. The wars were savage and bloody. But no matter how hard the Indians fought or how many battles they won, throughout the 18th and 19th centuries the white settlers kept coming, moving forever westward.

At first the whites thought that conquering the Santee Sioux of Minnesota would be an easy task compared with the brutal wars they had fought to subdue other Indian nations and tribes. It seemed, for a while, that the Santee Sioux had been removed as an obstacle without a shot being fired or an arrow launched in return. Starting in the early 1800s, the United States government simply "bought" the lands of the Santees. The deep woodlands of Minnesota, with thousands of lakes, rivers, and streams and seemingly endless supplies of lumber, wildlife, and fertile soil, were prized by the U.S. government and by white farmers, hunters, trappers, and traders. The government offered money and goods to the Indians in return for portions of Santee territory. But soon the government began demanding much more.

In 1837, a group of Santee chiefs, including Little Crow of the Mdewakantan Santees, were taken to Washington, D.C.

Little Crow, an important leader of the Santees, was one of the first to travel to Washington, see the size and strength of the white civilization there, and understand how impossible it would be for the Santees to preserve their lands and way of life. Still, he tried to resist the attack on his people's culture and led the famous Santee uprising of 1862.

There they saw firsthand the industrial power, technology, and, most of all, the booming population of the whites. When Little Crow returned home, he reported that the whites were too numerous to be counted and that their power was great. Their god, Little Crow reasoned, must be much greater than Wakan Tanka.

For Little Crow and many of the Santee leaders, there seemed to be little choice. Luke Lea, the commissioner of the Federal Bureau of Indian Affairs, explained the situation to Santee leaders at a treaty conference in 1849: "Suppose (the president) wanted your lands and did not want a treaty . . . he would come with 100,000 men and drive you off to the Rocky Mountains." For Little Crow and the other Santee leaders, the message was clear: either sell their lands to the whites and promise to remain peaceful, or have their lands taken by force. Besides, reasoned the Santees, surely there would be enough room for both peoples, for the country was huge, and the Santees would be selling only a part of their land. In return, they would receive many goods and much money, which could be used to buy more goods from the white traders who now flocked to Santee territory. But the Santees did not fully understand the hunger for property that drove the white Americans. In white society, property meant money, and money meant power.

The Santees soon learned that selling portions of their land would not keep the white Americans at bay. As the 19th century wore on, the white settlers kept coming. Soon, in order to open up new territories for the settlers, the U.S. government wanted to buy more Santee land. And by now the Santees were virtually powerless to withstand the invaders. For although the Santees knew that the whites threatened their very existence, they had become dependent on them.

The process had begun in the second half of the 17th century, when French and British traders first reached the Big Woods. In exchange for beaver furs obtained by Santee trappers, the traders offered money and goods such as steel knives, cotton and wool blankets and clothing, metal tools and hatchets and nails, attractive trinkets, firearms and ammunition, tobacco, coffee, and liquor. The European traders then shipped the beaver furs to Europe and sold them for a great profit. The beaver furs were made into fashionable items of clothing, such as hats, worn by wealthy Europeans.

By the time the Americans gained independence from England in the Revolutionary War and drove the British into Canada in the War of 1812, the Santees had come to depend on the money and goods they received from whites in return for furs. As a result, the new Americans could more easily buy the Santees' land.

Thus Santee culture had already become contaminated by the products of white culture. And the Santees had been contaminated in another way, too, for Europeans brought with them diseases such as smallpox, tuberculosis, and cholera. Because the Santees had never before been exposed to these diseases, their bodies were unable to resist them. The Santees were devastated by these diseases, with thousands dying. Like their homelands, the Santee population began to shrink. The population of white Americans, meanwhile, was exploding.

By the mid-19th century, many Santees began to realize that they had sold not only their lands, but their tribal soul as well. They could no longer range far and wide through the forests and across the meadows to hunt, for white settlers now owned those forests and meadows. In 1849, more than 20 million acres of Santee territory were sold to the United States in exchange for a narrow strip of territory along the Minnesota River—a reservation—and the promise of a yearly payment. Roughly 150,000 white settlers had come to the Big Woods, and they had no intention of leaving.

The great amount of money the Santees were supposed to receive each year as pay-

Charles Eastman, whose Santee name was Ohiyesa, grew up at a time when many Sioux were shedding their traditional culture. Although he attended white schools and later became a prominent doctor and writer, Eastman criticized the values of the white culture he had been obliged to adopt, saying that its motto was not "to be" but "to have."

ment for their lands seemed much smaller when it was divided among the entire tribe. And the federal government agents responsible for transferring the money to the Santees would first take a large portion for themselves. The money that finally made it into Santee hands was used to buy things such as food and blankets, and the white traders who sold these items to the Santees charged them outrageous sums.

The Santees now found themselves in a nightmarish situation: they had to depend on the government for food, clothing, and other items they needed to survive. The lands that still belonged to the Santees had little game left for hunting, and the soil had been overfarmed so that it was no longer fertile. Worse yet, the Santees were slowly but steadily being forced to abandon their traditional culture.

The U.S. government believed that the best way to handle the Indian "problem"— once a certain tribe had been defeated in combat or had lost its land and pride in the manner that the Santees had—was to turn the Indians into white people. The Santees were encouraged to cut their hair short, to wear white people's clothes, to speak English, to farm their land, to give up their own religion for Christianity. Those Santees who followed this path found that they got better deals from the traders and received more money—and received it on time— from the agents.

Many of the Santee Sioux attempted to please the government in this manner. But many others were angered by those who took up the ways of the white people and left behind traditional Santee culture. Many Santees were disgusted with themselves for behaving in this manner but felt that they had no choice. They needed their bacon and wool blankets and coffee—and, for some, their alcohol—and they depended on the whites for these things, even though they had never needed such things before the whites introduced them to the Santees.

Those Santees who refused to follow the white people's ways felt a growing contempt for the "white" Santees and for leaders such as Little Crow, who had sold their homeland out from under their feet. And those who chose to adopt the ways of the whites found that this did not win the respect of the whites. Although many white people and Indians were on friendly terms, most whites during this period considered Indians little more than a nuisance.

A deep hatred for the white Americans and a simmering anger and desperation were growing among the Santees. Whites had invaded Santee homelands, killed off the beaver, buffalo, deer, and wolf, introduced alchohol to make the Indians drunk and foolish, and chopped down the trees of the Big Woods. Santee chief Wabasha expressed the despair and anger of his people: "There is only one more thing that (the U.S. president) can do, and that is to gather us all together on the prairie and surround us with soldiers and shoot us down."

Some of the young Santee men had formed a warrior society, and they spoke of waging war on the whites and driving them from Minnesota. "The whites were always trying to make the Indians give up their ways and live like white men," said the Santee warrior Big Eagle. "If the Indians had tried to make the whites live like them, the whites would have resisted, and it was the same way with many Indians."

But most Santees were in awe of the whites and felt that such a thing would be impossible. In his book *Indian Boyhood*, published in 1902, Charles Eastman described how the Santee Sioux regarded the whites: "I had heard marvelous things of this people. In some things we despised them; in others we regarded them as wakan (mysterious), a race whose power bordered on the supernatural." In the summer of 1862, however, the Santee Sioux learned that white people were all too human. And the white Americans of Minnesota learned that the Santees had finally been pushed too far. ▲

CHAPTER 4

Andrew Myrick
Eats Grass

Some Santees were willing to adopt the white way of life encouraged by the federal government so took up farming, lived in brick houses, and wore white-style clothing. They were called "farmer Indians" by the other Santees, who resented this betrayal of traditional culture.

By the summer of 1862, the Santees were living in two groups on the ever-shrinking lands of their reservation. The four divisions of the Santee nation—the Wahpekutes, the Sissetons, the Wahpetons, and the Mdewakantons—had gradually settled around two agencies along the Minnesota River.

Agencies were places on reservations where Indians, government agents, priests, settlers, and traders interacted. They were small communities of houses, stores, trading posts, and usually at least one church.

45

A government-appointed Indian agent lived at each agency. Indian agents—who were almost always white men during this period—acted as administrators of the reservations.

Two agencies existed on the Santee reservation, with Santee villages scattered around and in between. They were known as the Upper Agency, located at the junction of the Minnesota and Yellow Medicine rivers, and the Lower Agency, located several miles up the Minnesota River from the Upper Agency, at a place called Redwood. The Wahpeton and Sisseton bands lived around the Upper Agency. The Mdewakanton and Wahpekute were settled around the Lower Agency.

The summer of 1862 was a bad time on the Santee reservation. The Santees were starving. They depended on the government for an *annuity*—the money and goods they were to be paid yearly for the sale of their lands and for their promise not to fight white settlers. The Santees needed this annuity to buy food and supplies from traders because by this time they had no other choice. The animals that the Santees had traditionally depended upon for food and for clothing had been hunted by both Indians and whites until they had virtually disappeared from the reservation. According to the treaties, the Santees could not leave the reservation to hunt. Those who did were not welcomed by the thousands of white settlers now populating the land that had once been Santee territory.

As the summer grew hotter, tensions on the reservation increased. June came and went without the annuity payments. A warehouse at the Upper Agency was stocked with food and supplies, but the Indian agent, Major Thomas Galbraith, would not open the warehouse until the annuity shipment had arrived and the Santees had money to buy supplies. He told the Indians to hunt for their food, although he knew there was nothing left to hunt on the reservation. By July, some infants and elderly Indians had died of starvation.

Not all of the Santee were starving, however. Those Santees—known as "farmer Indians"—who had accepted the government's attempts to make them "white," were eating quite well. Galbraith supplied them with generous amounts of food from the storehouse. The farmer Indians had converted to Christianity, dressed like white people, and farmed the soil like white farmers. The "blanket Indians"—those who refused to give up traditional Santee culture and values—despised these "white" Indians. Farmer Indians were frequently threatened, harassed, attacked, and even killed by the blanket Indians. This hostility contributed to the rising tensions on the Santee reservation, and when the annuity failed to arrive that June many rebellious Santees began meeting in secret to discuss attacking the whites.

On June 20, several Santee chiefs and leaders, led by Chief Little Crow, held a meeting with Agent Galbraith and four traders at the Redwood agency. Little Crow pleaded with Galbraith to open the storehouse for all the Santees, and he gave the agent an ominous warning: "When men are hungry they help themselves." Galbraith discussed the situation with the traders. One of them, Andrew Myrick, commented, "So far as I am concerned, if they are hungry, let them eat grass." Hearing this, the Indians departed angrily.

The Upper Agency, where the stores of food were kept, was now surrounded by 5,000 starving Santees. They sat and waited, sick with hunger, their protruding ribs showing how little they had eaten over the past months. Galbraith summoned 100 U.S. Army soldiers from Fort Ridgely, 40 miles to the southeast, to protect the

continued on page 57

THE ART OF THE PLAINS

Like other Plains Indians, the Santee Sioux were known for their careful needlework, using porcupine quills and glass beads to turn shoes, clothing, and accessories into beautiful keepsakes.

Before the 18th century, Santee women sewed brightly dyed porcupine quills onto leather surfaces, tying the quills together so that they looked like continuous strands of color. Blue, pink, yellow, white, and green hues—derived from vegetables and minerals—were favorite colors for Santee quillwork.

At the beginning of the 18th century, European traders introduced a new medium for colorful artwork: tiny glass beads. They gave these "pony beads" to the Santees as gifts or in exchange for skins and furs. By the mid-19th century, Santee craftswomen had for the most part stopped using pony beads in favor of smaller, more elongated "seed beads" imported from Venice and Czechoslovakia. The different size and shape of seed beads changed Santee beadwork dramatically; pony beads had been scattered throughout larger designs, but now artisans created designs featuring entire surfaces covered with beads.

Today, very few people are skilled quillworkers. Beadwork continues in the Plains region, however, and extraordinary examples of both crafts survive to provide us with a hint of the great scope of Santee creativity.

Santee moccasins with intricate beadwork, circa 1900.

A fringed deerskin jacket with beadwork depictions of rattlesnakes, various birds, and a turtle. The jacket was made for a white man, J. F. Lenger, probably by Nebraska Santee women, circa 1890.

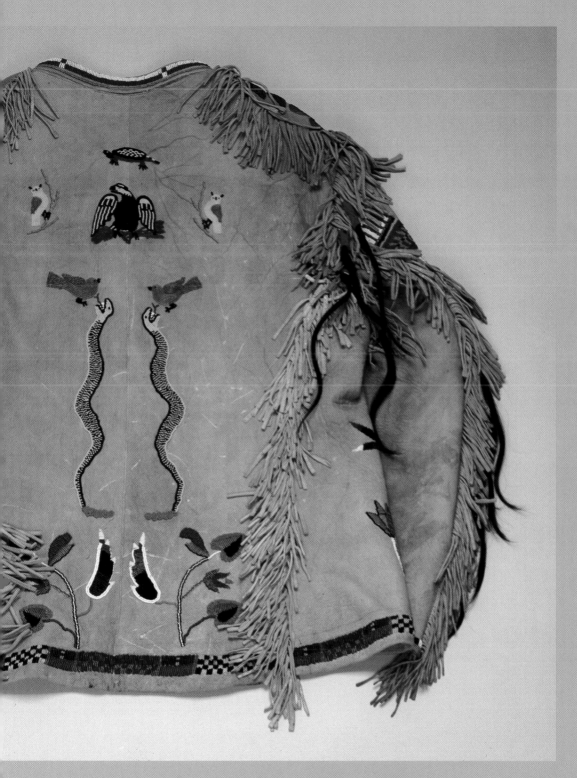

Fringed deerskin pants, also made for J. F. Lenger, circa 1890.

52

Deerskin vest with beadwork design, circa 1900.

A bandolier bag. Worn across one shoulder, it rested on the opposite hip.

54

A pair of leggings, or horse chaps, designed to protect the pants. They were slipped over the pants from the ankle to the knee and were tied with the leather cord.

Santee bag with porcupine-quill design, circa 1900. Bright pink was a favorite color in Santee designs.

continued from page 48

agency and the storehouse. He instructed Lieutenant Timothy Sheehan, who was in command of the troops, to place them in a protective circle around the storehouse.

Just before dawn on August 4, 1862, 800 mounted Santee warriors thundered down on the Yellow Medicine Agency. In full war paint and dress, they circled the troops and the storehouse, firing guns into the air and whooping and shouting. Then they stopped and gathered together before the door to the brick storehouse. They were confronted by the soldiers blocking the entrance, and a silent standoff began. Both groups held their weapons at the ready and stared at one another, waiting for the first rifle shot or hissing arrow that would ignite a battle.

But Lieutenant Sheehan was either a very wise or a very fair man. Perhaps he was both. In order to prevent what could only result in extreme bloodshed, he convinced Galbraith to distribute some food from the storehouse. When this was done, the Santee warriors rode off. Because the crisis seemed to have passed, the soldiers returned to Fort Ridgely. But the food was not nearly enough to feed the thousands of starving Santees. August stretched on, and still the annuity did not arrive.

On Sunday, August 17, four young Santees from the Lower Agency, their stomachs rumbling with hunger, went out to attempt to hunt. But after many hours they had found nothing, so with empty hands and empty bellies they began the 40-mile journey back to their settlement. Along the way they passed the land of Mr. and Mrs. Robinson Jones. Mr. Jones was a farmer who made a profitable extra income by selling whiskey to the Santees. The disastrous effects of liquor on Indian society were already well known, but whites such as Jones continued to make money off the growing numbers of alcoholic Indians. Many Santees consequently disliked Jones for selling alcohol to an already desperate people.

As they crossed Jones's pastures, the four Santees came across a hen's nest. The nest contained some eggs, and one of the Santees started to take them. Another cautioned him, saying that they might get in trouble for stealing. "You are a coward," the first Santee shouted. "You are afraid of the white man. You are afraid to take even an egg from him, even though you are half starved!"

The other Santee, starving, desperate, and angry, replied that he was no coward. To

In exchange for giving up vast areas of land for hunting, Sioux Indians relied on the government to deliver the money, food supplies, and clothing that had been promised. Here Sioux families wait to receive their rations from government agents.

prove it, he said, he would go and kill the white people living in the nearby cabin. The other Indians said they would go with him. And with that, they headed over to the Joneses' cabin.

At first, the young Santees demanded food from Jones. Jones brusquely told them that he had no food to spare and, taking his rifle and ignoring the four Indians, walked over to the cabin of his relatives, the Bakers. Jones's wife was at the Bakers' place, visiting her son, Howard Baker, his

wife, and their two children. A friend of Howard Baker, named Webster, was there as well.

The four Santees followed Jones to the Bakers' cabin, where one of the Indians proposed a shooting contest. Jones, Webster, and Baker shot first, using a tree stump as a target. When the Santees' turn to shoot came, they all aimed at the target. Then, suddenly, they turned on Robinson Jones and shot him. The Santees then shot down the other three, who were taken completely by surprise and had no chance to defend themselves. The four Santees fled, stealing horses from another farm, and reached their village near the Lower Agency by nightfall.

There the four young men were asked again and again to tell their story. In fact, the Santees at the village were more interested in the details of the killings and in how easily the whites had been killed than in the fact that, if caught, the young Indians involved would surely be hanged.

News of the killings had soon spread throughout the Lower Agency. A meeting was called at the house of Chief Little Crow, and the hundreds of Santee warriors who gathered there argued for hours over what to do next. Most wanted to declare war immediately. They would all suffer for the

Chief Little Crow sold a great deal of the Santees' land to the government because he felt he had no choice. Nevertheless, when the government failed to provide the payment and supplies it had promised, Little Crow agreed to lead the attack on white settlers that became known as the great Sioux uprising of 1862.

murders, they reasoned, so why not do what they should have done years ago— drive every white man, woman, and child from their land? Now was the time: the whites were weak, as most of their soldiers were off fighting in the Civil War. So if the Santees attacked now they would surprise the settlers. It was better than waiting for the soldiers to come and demand that the Santees hand over the four young murderers.   It was better than starving like dogs. Besides, the warrior Red Middle Voice reminded them, "We have no choice.   Our hands are already bloody."

The Santee warriors wanted Little Crow to lead them against the whites.   But he was against war: he had been to Washington, had seen the great numbers of white men, and had heard the roar of the army's cannons.   "The white men are like locusts when they fly so thick the whole sky is a snowstorm," he told the gathered warriors.   "You may kill one—two—ten, and ten times ten will come to kill you."

At this, Red Middle Voice walked over to where Little Crow sat, looked down at him, and said, "Little Crow is a coward."   For Little Crow had been one of the chiefs who had signed away Santee lands in treaties with the whites, and he was almost a farmer Indian himself.   He lived in a brick house, ate at a table with chairs, and even dressed like a white man.   But Red Middle Voice knew that if Little Crow led them, their numbers would be doubled, for many who were undecided about what to do would follow the chief if he went to war.   Many farmer Indians might shed their white man's clothes and join the warriors.   To goad him, Red Middle Voice said, "Little Crow is afraid of the white man." At this Little Crow rose to his feet. "Little Crow is no coward," he replied. "I will die with you like a Sioux."

The rebellious Santees first attacked the Lower Agency, where they set fire to the houses and stores and killed most of the traders, officials, and missionaries. Many warriors gathered around the house and store of the trader Andrew Myrick, who had told the starving Santees to "eat grass." They shot bullets and arrows through the windows and then set the building on fire. Myrick, wounded, fled upstairs, clambered through a back window, and tried to climb down a tree. By the time he reached the ground he was so full of arrows he looked like a porcupine, and many bullets found him as he tried to crawl away. After he was dead, one of the warriors stuffed a handful of grass into his mouth. "Who eats grass now?" angry Santees demanded of the dead man again and again as they destroyed the Redwood Agency around Myrick's body. Fire and smoke from burning buildings climbed into the sky, and the bodies of about 20 white people lay scattered about the packed-earth roads. The great Sioux uprising of 1862 had begun. ▲

This illustration, which appeared in Harper's New Monthly Magazine, *shows a white artist's interpretation of the Santee uprising.*

CHAPTER 5

"Over the Earth I Come"

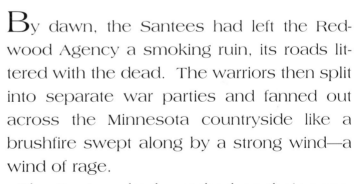

By dawn, the Santees had left the Red-wood Agency a smoking ruin, its roads littered with the dead. The warriors then split into separate war parties and fanned out across the Minnesota countryside like a brushfire swept along by a strong wind—a wind of rage.

The Santees had watched as their once-proud culture was reduced to a shadow of itself by a race of invaders. Many Santees now believed that the time had passed to watch and wait for white people to supply them with food, with new gods, with all-important money, with destructive alcohol, and with shabby farmer's clothes as their own culture, traditions, and land were taken away. Now it was time for war.

Because of the relative ease with which so many of the Santees had yielded their land, way of life, and pride as an independent people, nobody expected the events of 1862. Most white citizens of Minnesota considered the Santees to be dispirited and passive. Even those who were warned ahead of time—either by other settlers or by friendly Santees—refused to believe that the Santees were killing white people. Many who should have fled chose to remain on

Settlers who escaped the Santee uprising of 1862 had been taken completely by surprise. Although at least 400 white people were killed in the fighting, the Santees spared many with whom they had friendly relations.

their farms or settlements and were taken by surprise. Even some of those who fled found that it was too late. Helen Carruthers, with her family and several other white families—about 30 people in all—tried to reach the protection of Fort Ridgely. But the three wagons carrying them were overtaken by 70 Santee warriors. Mrs. Carruthers, who had a long and extremely friendly relationship with the Santees, pleaded for her life and for the lives of the people with her. She was spared, taken prisoner along with several other women and children. Everyone else, however, was killed.

By noon, word of the uprising had reached Fort Ridgely, where refugees, many of them wounded and all of them terrified, were arriving. They all told tales of slaughter. Captain John Marsh, the officer in charge of the fort, gathered together 46 soldiers and set out to crush the rebellion—a brave but foolish action. Marsh underestimated the scope of the uprising. His small force was ambushed along the banks of the Minnesota River, and Marsh himself drowned attempting to swim across the river to safety. Only a handful of survivors from Marsh's company made it back to the fort.

As night fell, the sky above the Big Woods glowed orange with the flames of burning fields, barns, and houses, and smoke filled the Minnesota River valley.   About 400 whites had been killed and 100 taken prisoner by the Santee war parties that seemed to be everywhere. The entire white population of the Minnesota territory was in flight. Hundreds of refugees continued to pour into Fort Ridgely.

Lieutenant Thomas Gere was now in command, and he believed that the Santees would eventually attack the fort. He dispatched a messenger to the nearest U.S. Army post with a letter begging for reinforcements. Then he began planning to defend Fort Ridgely.

On the first night of the uprising, Little Crow and the other Santee leaders and important warriors gathered at Little Crow's camp to debate what to do next. Many of the chiefs and warriors had only contempt for those Santees who had spent the day killing women and children, which they thought was a cowardly way of fighting and not worthy of a Sioux. Little Crow agreed. The Santees, he said, should wage war against the U.S. soldiers, not civilians. He wanted to attack Fort Ridgely. It was poorly defended, according to his scouts, and the Santees could take it easily if they organized a massed attack. Soon, they knew, more

In the end, the uprising of 1862 only hurt the Santees more, causing them to lose the remaining rights to their homeland. The wife and children of Little Crow are pictured here at Fort Snelling, where even those Santees who did not take part in the violence were held before being sent to the Dakota badlands.

U.S. troops would arrive to crush the rebellion. But if Fort Ridgely were taken and held with its supplies and cannon, the Santees could fend off the army until a favorable treaty was signed. As Big Eagle said, "It was of the greatest importance for us to take the fort. If we could take it we would soon have the whole Minnesota Valley."

On Wednesday morning at dawn, Little Crow led a force of 400 warriors toward Fort Ridgely. Lieutenant Timothy Sheehan meanwhile reached the fort with about 50 soldiers and took command from Gere. At two o'clock that afternoon, the Santees arrived at the fort as well, and the attack began.

A fierce battle followed. The defenders of the fort were greatly outnumbered; no more than 200 soldiers and about 20 civilian volunteers were available to fight off the Santees. Yet despite repeated charges and bloody fighting near the gates to the fort, the Santees could not penetrate to the center of the post. Lieutenants Gere and Sheehan and their men fought heroically, and the 300 refugees were protected in a brick warehouse. The six artillery pieces within the fort were expertly placed. Again and again the charges of the Sioux were halted by the blasts of the big guns. Late in the afternoon, the Santees broke off their attack and returned to Little Crow's camp.

The Santees attacked again the next morning. This time, Little Crow commanded a force of 800 warriors. Throughout the previous night, the forces of the Sioux had grown as bands of Santees returned from their raiding in the Big Woods. Most of the Upper Agency Santees, who so far had refused to join forces with Little Crow, now put on war paint and rode into his camp. Many farmer Indians replaced their overalls and hoes with war paint, bows and arrows, tomahawks, rifles, and other weapons and joined the force of warriors. They chanted a Santee war song as they advanced on the fort at sunrise: "Over the earth I come, over the earth I come. . . ."

Lieutenant Sheehan had also spent the night preparing for another attack. The walls of the fort had been reinforced, and barricades had been set up inside. The second attack on Fort Ridgely turned into a bloody, day-long battle. Hand-to-hand combat raged around the outer buildings of the fort, but again the attacks of the Sioux were driven back by cannon fire. By sundown, the Santees had had enough, and they withdrew.

The next day, changing strategies, the Santees swept down on the large town of New Ulm, where a corps of volunteer citizens battled them in the streets and inside houses. Although the Sioux failed to capture the town, they left it in burning ruins with many of the defenders dead or wounded.

By now, the Minnesota territory was beginning to receive reinforcements. Although an army of 1,200 soldiers was marching on the Sioux, Little Crow stubbornly continued the war, ambushing columns of soldiers. But the Sioux knew that their uprising was now a lost cause: the failure to take Fort Ridgely had doomed them. As armies of U.S. soldiers arrived, it was clear that the uprising was over. ◭

Eventually some Santees returned to their old homeland in Minnesota—although by then both it and they had changed. Here Sioux schoolchildren are shown in their classroom at the Lower Sioux Agency in Morton, Minnesota, in about 1900. By this time the clothing, language, beliefs, setting, and even role models of a young Santee were identical to those of a white child.

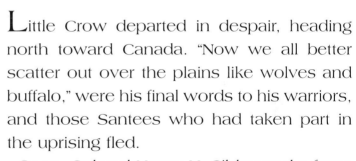

CHAPTER 6

"Like Wolves and Buffalo"

Little Crow departed in despair, heading north toward Canada. "Now we all better scatter out over the plains like wolves and buffalo," were his final words to his warriors, and those Santees who had taken part in the uprising fled.

Soon, Colonel Henry H. Sibley and a force of 1,200 soldiers were in control of the region, and the Santees who remained near the agencies—most of whom had not participated in the uprising—found themselves surrounded as prisoners of war. Sibley sent out troops to capture those Santees who were on the run. Indeed, like "wolves and buffalo" they were hunted down.

White America was outraged by the uprising. The Santees must be "removed or exterminated," cried politicians such as Minnesota governor Alexander Ramsey. Trials, imprisonments, and hangings began. In the end, the Santee uprising of 1862 accomplished nothing but bloodshed and further suffering for the Santees. It also provided the American government with an excuse to do what it had wanted to do all along: remove the Santees from Minnesota altogether and claim the former Santee Sioux homelands as United States property. Most of the remaining Sioux were shipped to their new reservation at desolate Crow Creek.

There, like the wolf and the buffalo, the Santees hovered on the brink of extinction. In order to keep Santees from returning to Minnesota and to eliminate any who might have stayed, the government paid $75 to anyone turning in the scalp of a Santee— proof that a Santee had been killed. The U.S. Army continued to hunt bands of Santees who had fled onto the Great Plains. Several battles between U.S. troops and groups of Santees occurred in the western Teton Sioux country—the battles of Big Mound, Dead Buffalo Lake, Stoney Lake, and Whitestone Hill, in North Dakota—and were won by the U.S. soldiers. But few Sioux warriors were killed or captured. They usually fled with their women and children after they ran out of ammunition, disappearing into the wilderness or taking refuge among the Teton Sioux. These battles scattered the Santee tribe even further.

Despite the outcome of the uprising, Little Crow and his small band of followers were determined to continue the war against the U.S. After hiding in Canada for a while, they slipped back into Minnesota and began attacking settlements. On June 3, 1863, while picking raspberries, Little Crow was shot and killed by a settler. The farmer was given a $500 reward for his action, and Little Crow's skeleton was put on display at the St. Paul, Minnesota, Historical Society. Two other Santee leaders who had participated in the uprising—Shakopee and Medicine Bottle—fled to Canada following their defeat. In 1864 they were hunted down by U.S. agents, kidnapped, brought back to the United States, and hanged.

Eventually, hostilities ceased. Many bands of Santees turned themselves over to the U.S. government. The day of the Santees was over. They had scattered far and wide, and it seemed that they would never again live together as the Santee Sioux nation.

By the turn of the century, America was the white people's country. The few remaining Santee Sioux were living desperate lives in widespread locations. The Crow Creek Santees had been moved to a reservation in Nebraska, where they attempted to live as farmers and where many had converted to Christianity. Another band of Sioux, originally from the Upper Agency, settled at the Coteau Des Prairies area near Big Stone Lake in Dakota Territory. Eventually, the government granted these Santees two reservations: Devil's Lake Reservation and Fort Wadsworth Reservation. In Flandreau, South Dakota, a band of Santees formed their own settlement. And, remarkably, as the years passed, small bands of Santees slipped back into Minnesota and formed small settlements throughout the state.

As the 20th century progressed, the reservations and settlements of the Santees and other Native American tribes became islands in a sea of white American towns, highways, and cities. For the Santees, preserving elements of their traditional culture became almost impossible. Most of the Santees were struggling merely to survive.

Many Santees attempted to take on the ways of the whites and to *assimilate*

This 1900 photograph shows Sioux women who might once have painted red dots on their foreheads or adorned their deerskin clothing with shells, now employed as lace makers. Although these women have taken on many of the trappings of white society, they still wear the hairstyles—and even the moccasins—of traditional Sioux women.

themselves into white American society. But this proved difficult. Some Santees became successful farmers and ranchers. Others obtained government-appointed jobs on the reservations. Some, such as

Charles Eastman, succeeded in American society as professionals. Mostly, however, the Santees continued to depend on the government for their welfare. As a result, the Santees often lived in the most desperate state of poverty. On the reservations, disease, despair, unemployment, alcoholism, suicide, and dismal living conditions took a heavy toll. Most of those who ventured off the reservations became victims of discrimination and prejudice in the white world, and many found it impossible to join America's work force. At times, the populations of various reservations and settlements slipped so low that the inhabitants truly seemed to face extinction.

The 1960s, however, brought hope for the Santee Sioux. An influx of federal aid resulted in new housing and roads in Santee settlements and reservations. Major industries rising on or near reservations provided jobs, and many reservations opened casinos or bingo parlors, providing more jobs and tribal income.

Most importantly, a sense of tribal and spiritual renewal began spreading throughout the reservations. Schools, including junior colleges designed specifically for Native Americans, were founded on or near reservations and villages. Many of these schools

Since the 1960s the Sioux and other Native Americans have experienced a sense of tribal and spiritual renewal. Here two children wear traditional ceremonial dress to take part in a powwow in 1972.

emphasize tribal history and culture and are taught by American Indians who have graduated from major colleges and returned to the reservations to help their people.

As a new century approaches, the Santees have found that their traditional culture gives them pride and a renewed sense of individual and community strength. Today, a Santee can work at the local power plant, for example, and still practice Santee traditions and the tribal spirituality that the government and the early Christian missionaries had tried so hard to eliminate. On some reservations, the Santees are returning to tribal, rather than individual, ownership of their land.   This is happening on many other Indian reservations as well.

Furthermore, the general population of non-Indian Americans—especially young non-Indian Americans—is showing an avid interest in the histories and cultures of the original American nations and tribes. Non-Indian writers, historians, sociologists, teachers, artists, and students are developing a new empathy for the devastation suffered by the original Americans. And, in a most ironic turn of events, many non-Indian Americans are now turning to traditional Indian culture and spirituality. Many of today's non-Indian Americans hope that

Native American ideas and beliefs will provide answers to the problems threatening the United States as another century approaches—pollution, the destruction of the natural environment, and a loss of a sense of true spirituality and national community.

For many Santee Sioux, the 21st century holds hope and the promise of renewal. Using today's communication technology and yesterday's sense of tribal community, the Santees look forward to the time when the scattered people become a single nation once again—and benefit the entire American community. ▲

GLOSSARY

annuity an annual payment of money or goods

assimilation a process in which a people such as the Santees abandon their own way of life and instead adopt that of another people

Bill of Rights the first nine amendments to the Constitution, added in 1791 to ensure personal liberties

capital punishment the penalty of death for certain crimes

Constitution the document of 1787 that contains the principles on which the United States government is based

giveaway a Santee custom in which a person celebrating an important event (such as a birth or marriage) makes gifts to friends and family

isanti the Sioux word for knife, from which the Santee got their name because they camped near Knife Lake

reservation a piece of public land set aside for Native American tribes

tiyospaye the extended family unit in Santee society

Wakan Tanka the "Great Mysterious," or supreme life force in Sioux religious belief

CHRONOLOGY

1660s   Santees begin to exchange furs for metal implements and weapons from French traders

late 1700s   Santees have replaced many of their traditional tools and goods with those supplied by white traders; the continent becomes the domain of the new United States

1805   Santees have first contact with a representative of the United States government, Lieutenant Zebulon Pike, who buys 100,000 acres of their land for $2,000

1837   Santee delegation travels to Washington and signs treaty selling to the U.S. government all lands east of the Mississippi

1849   Through treaty signed at Traverse des Sioux, Santees sell 21 million acres of land for a small reservation and the promise of an annual payment of money and goods

1854   Chief Little Crow travels to Washington, where he is told that his people may remain on their lands forever

1858   Again Little Crow and other chiefs travel to Washington, where threats make them yield still more land for supplies

1862   When promised supplies fail to arrive from the government, desperate Santees stage an attack known as the Sioux uprising of 1862, for which 38 Santees are later hanged

1863   Santees are removed from the Minnesota region and taken to live in the Dakota badlands

1868   Santee leaders negotiate with the government for permanent reservations

c.1900   Having been scattered across the Northwest, most Santees have abandoned their traditional way of life and become Christians

1960s   After years of struggling with poverty, disease, and unemployment, Santees finally begin to experience economic improvement and a new sense of tribal community

INDEX

ABOUT THE AUTHOR

TERRANCE DOLAN is the editor of numerous books for young readers and the author of *The Kiowa Indians* in the Chelsea House series JUNIOR LIBRARY OF AMERICAN INDIANS and of *Probing Deep Space* in Chelsea House's WORLD EXPLORERS series.

PICTURE CREDITS